COLOR THE SHAPES

50 GEOMETRIC PATTERNS AND DESIGNS

BY STEPHANIE SANCHEZ

FREE COLORING BOOK

If you would like to get 10 extra free coloring pages, go to the link below or scan the QR code

https://bit.ly/3lMdNcd

IGNORE IF YOU'RE COLORING WITH MARKERS
IF NOT, TAKE A BREAK WITH THESE FUN FACTS

FACT:
THE FIRST ORANGES WEREN'T ORANGE

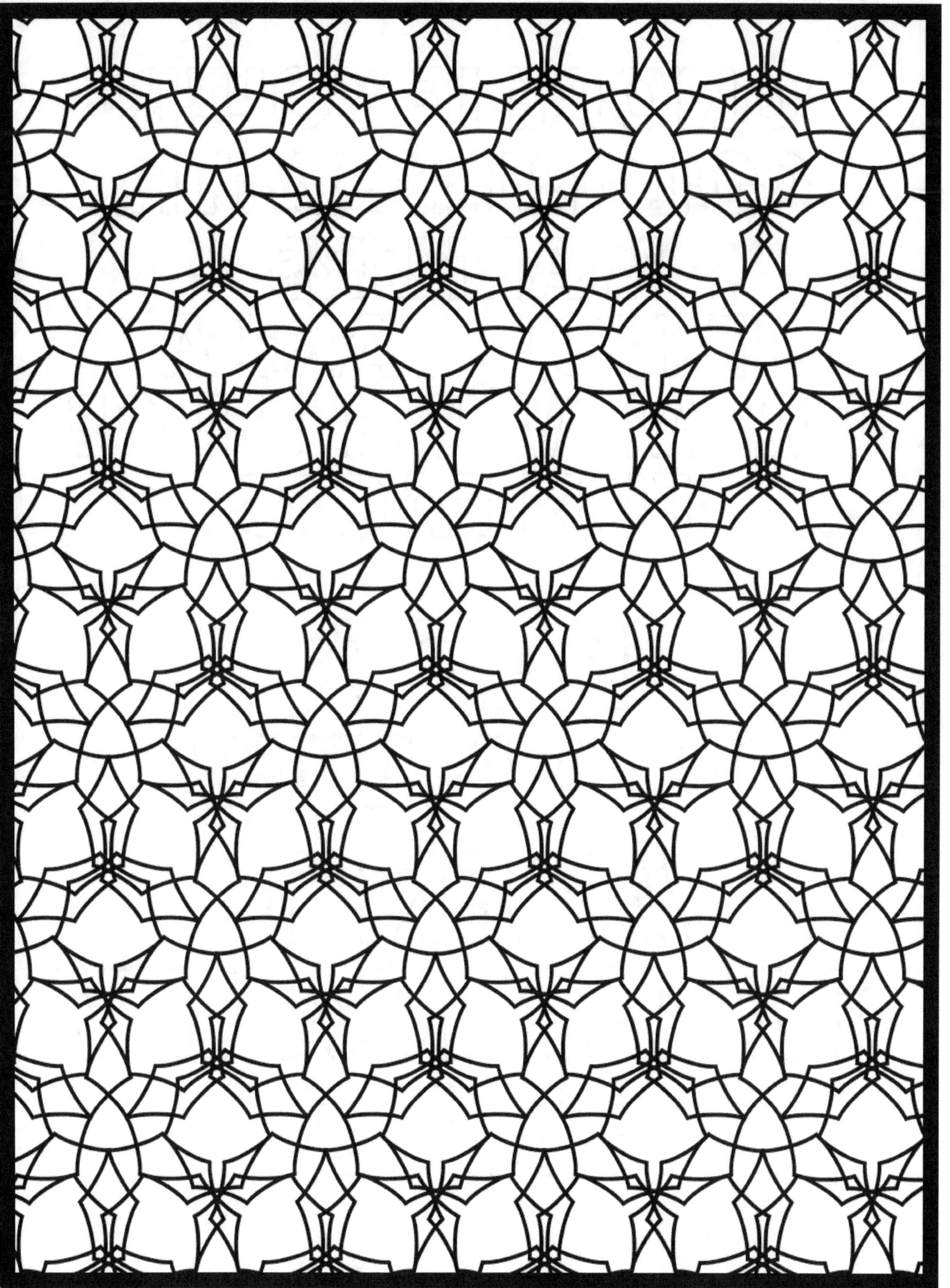

IGNORE IF YOU'RE COLORING WITH MARKERS
IF NOT, TAKE A BREAK WITH THESE FUN FACTS

FACT: PEANUTS AREN'T TECHNICALLY NUTS

IGNORE IF YOU'RE COLORING WITH MARKERS
IF NOT, TAKE A BREAK WITH THESE FUN FACTS
FACT:
ARMADILLO SHELLS ARE BULLETPROOF

IGNORE IF YOU'RE COLORING WITH MARKERS.
IF NOT, TAKE A BREAK WITH THESE FUN FACTS

FACT: BLUE WHALES EAT HALF A MILLION CALORIES IN ONE MOUTHFUL

IGNORE IF YOU'RE COLORING WITH MARKERS.

IF NOT, TAKE A BREAK WITH THESE FUN FACTS

FACT: COWS DON'T HAVE UPPER FRONT TEETH

IGNORE IF YOU'RE COLORING WITH MARKERS.

IF NOT, TAKE A BREAK WITH THESE FUN FACTS

FACT: NO NUMBER BEFORE 1,000 CONTAINS THE LETTER A

IGNORE IF YOU'RE COLORING WITH MARKERS.

IF NOT, TAKE A BREAK WITH THESE FUN FACTS

FACT: NO NUMBER BEFORE 1,000 CONTAINS THE LETTER A

IGNORE IF YOU'RE COLORING WITH MARKERS.

IF NOT, TAKE A BREAK WITH THESE FUN FACTS

FACT: CROWS CAN HOLD GRUDGES AGAINST SPECIFIC INDIVIDUAL PEOPLE

IGNORE IF YOU'RE COLORING WITH MARKERS.

IF NOT, TAKE A BREAK WITH THESE FUN FACTS

FACT: 7% OF AMERICAN ADULTS BELIEVE THAT CHOCOLATE MILK COMES FROM BROWN COWS

IGNORE IF YOU'RE COLORING WITH MARKERS.

IF NOT, TAKE A BREAK WITH THESE FUN FACTS

FACT: BANANAS ARE CURVED BECAUSE THEY GROW TOWARDS THE SUN

IGNORE IF YOU'RE COLORING WITH MARKERS.

IF NOT, TAKE A BREAK WITH THESE FUN FACTS

FACT: AN EAGLE CAN HUNT DOWN A YOUNG DEER AND FLY AWAY WITH IT

IGNORE IF YOU'RE COLORING WITH MARKERS.

IF NOT, TAKE A BREAK WITH THESE FUN FACTS

FACT: THE SMALLEST BONE IN YOUR BODY IS YOUR EAR

IGNORE IF YOU'RE COLORING WITH MARKERS.

IF NOT, TAKE A BREAK WITH THESE FUN FACTS

FACT: THE BIGGEST ORGAN IN THE HUMAN BODY IS THE SKIN

IGNORE IF YOU'RE COLORING WITH MARKERS.

IF NOT, TAKE A BREAK WITH THESE FUN FACTS

FACT: A LION'S ROAR CAN BE HEARD FROM 5 MILES AWAY

IGNORE IF YOU'RE COLORING WITH MARKERS.

IF NOT, TAKE A BREAK WITH THESE FUN FACTS

FACT: RECYCLING ONE GLASS JAR SAVES ENOUGH ENERGY TO WATCH TELEVISION FOR 3 HOURS

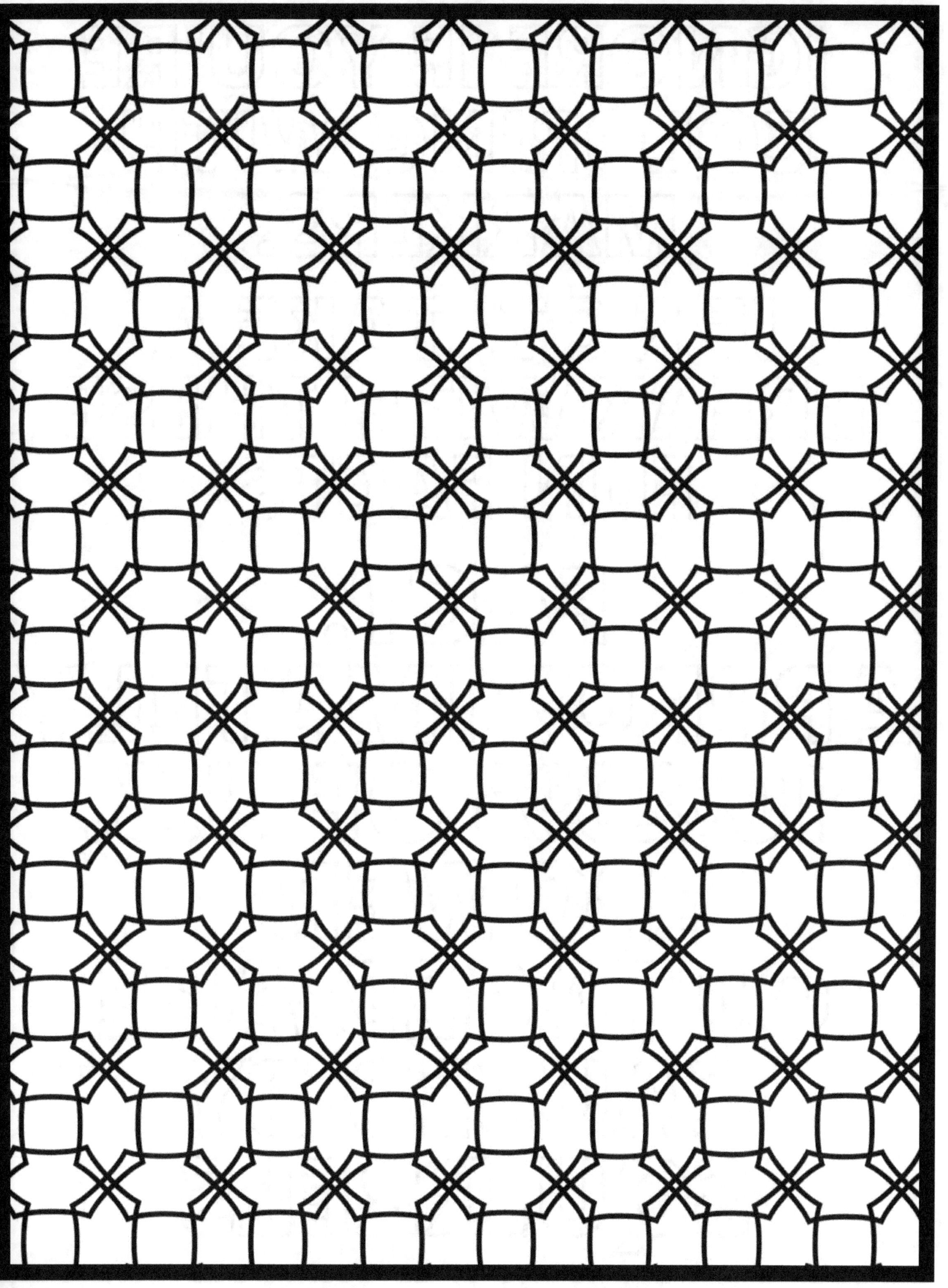

IGNORE IF YOU'RE COLORING WITH MARKERS.

IF NOT, TAKE A BREAK WITH THESE FUN FACTS

FACT:
APPROXIMATELY 10-20% OF U.S. POWER OUTAGED ARE CAUSED BY SQUIRRELS

IGNORE IF YOU'RE COLORING WITH MARKERS.

IF NOT, TAKE A BREAK WITH THESE FUN FACTS

FACT: HONEYBEES CAN RECOGNIZE HUMAN FACES

IGNORE IF YOU'RE COLORING WITH MARKERS.

IF NOT, TAKE A BREAK WITH THESE FUN FACTS

FACT: EATING CARROTS CAN TURN YOUR SKIN ORANGE

IGNORE IF YOU'RE COLORING WITH MARKERS.

IF NOT, TAKE A BREAK WITH THESE FUN FACTS

FACT: A CROCODILE CAN'T POKE ITS TONGUE OUT

IGNORE IF YOU'RE COLORING WITH MARKERS.

IF NOT, TAKE A BREAK WITH THESE FUN FACTS

FACT: DURING YOUR LIFETIME, YOU WILL SPEND AROUND 38 DAYS BRUSHING YOUR TEETH

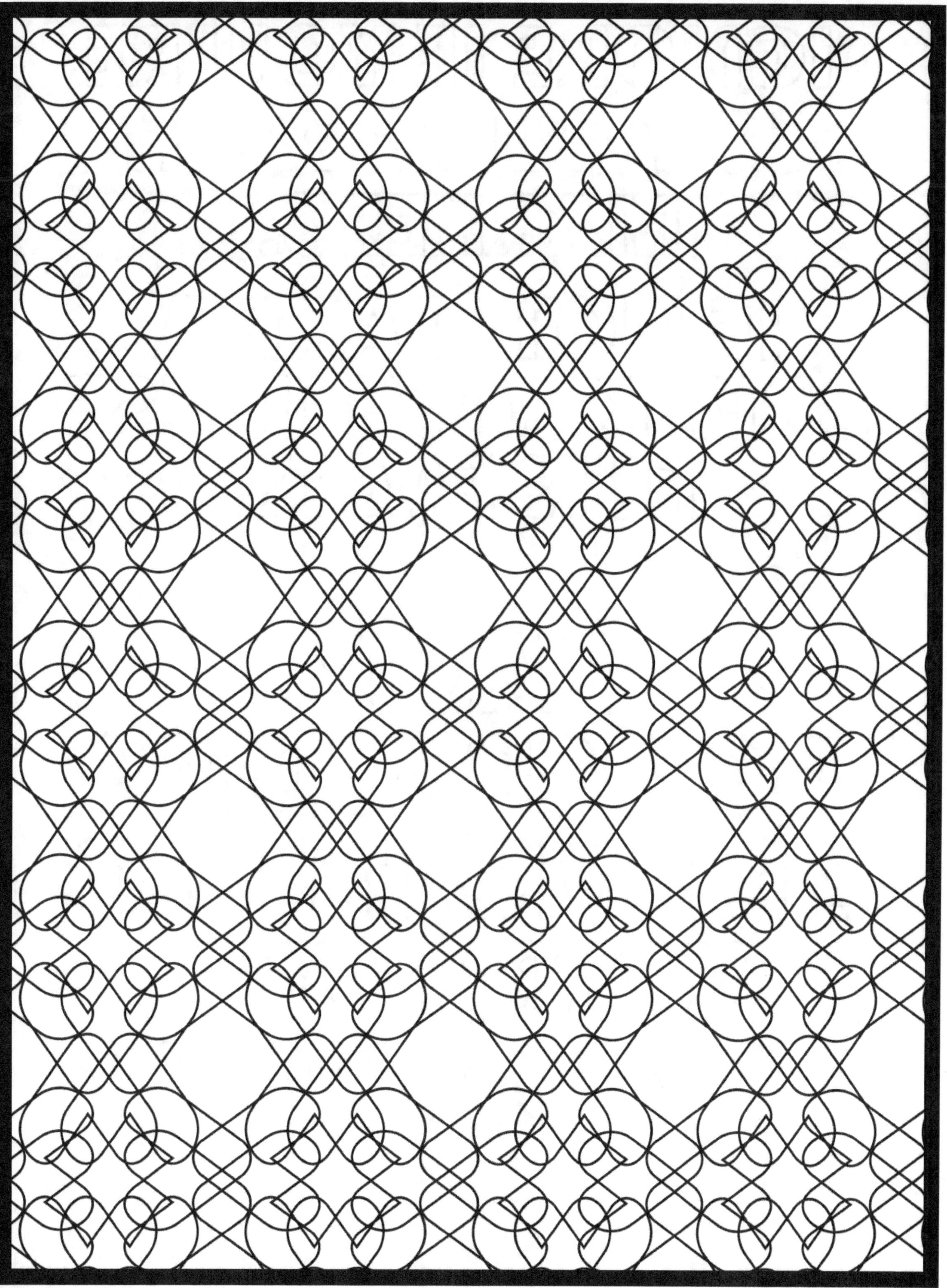

IGNORE IF YOU'RE COLORING WITH MARKERS.

IF NOT, TAKE A BREAK WITH THESE FUN FACTS

FACT: GOOSEBUMPS ARE MEANT TO WARD OFF PREDATORS

IGNORE IF YOU'RE COLORING WITH MARKERS.

IF NOT, TAKE A BREAK WITH THESE FUN FACTS

FACT: COTTON CANDY WAS INVENTED BY A DENTIST

IGNORE IF YOU'RE COLORING WITH MARKERS.

IF NOT, TAKE A BREAK WITH THESE FUN FACTS

FACT: CHEWING GUMS BOOSTS CONCENTRATION

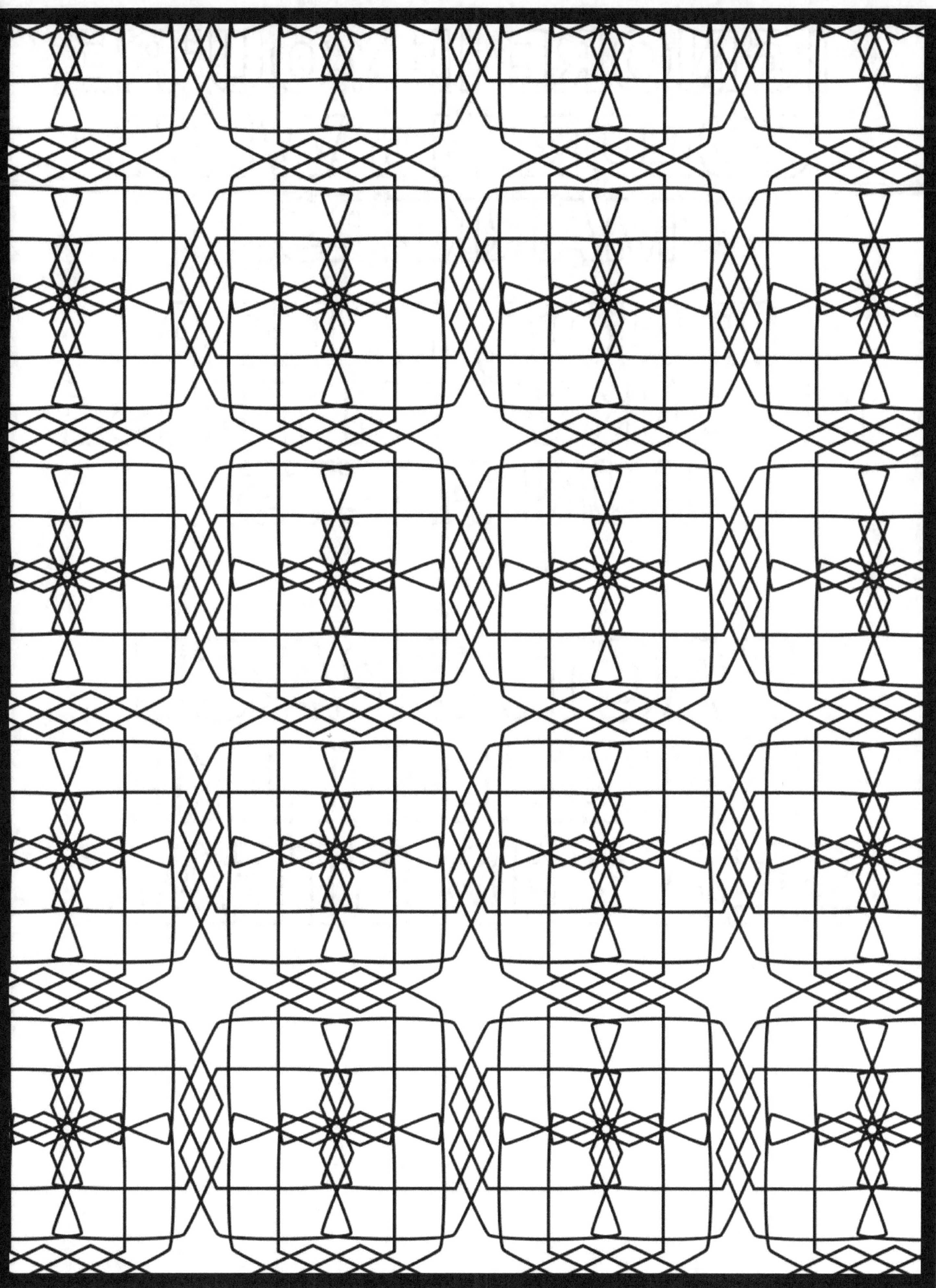

IGNORE IF YOU'RE COLORING WITH MARKERS.

IF NOT, TAKE A BREAK WITH THESE FUN FACTS

FACT: SPACE SMELLS LIKE SEARED STEAK

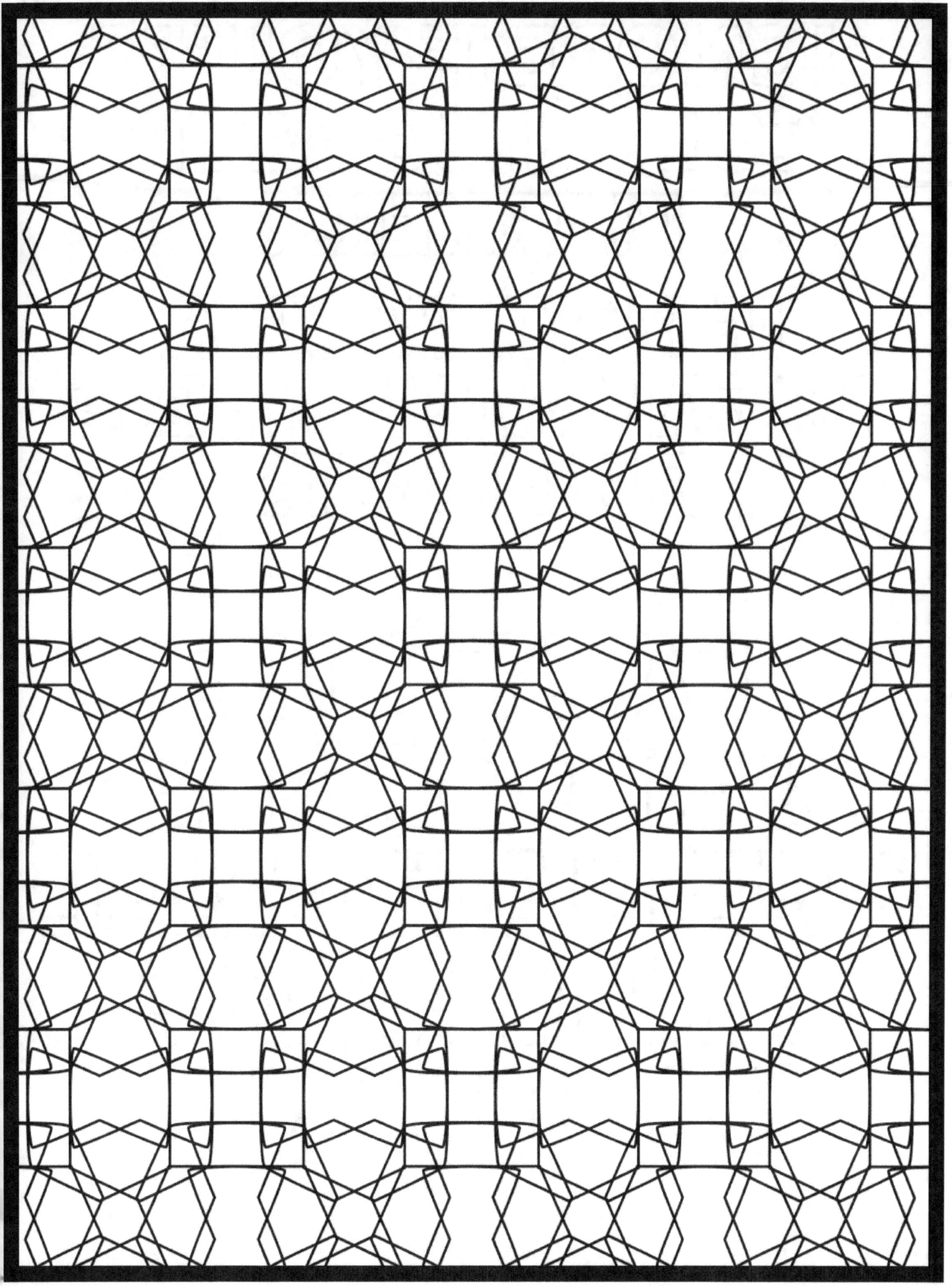

IGNORE IF YOU'RE COLORING WITH MARKERS.

IF NOT, TAKE A BREAK WITH THESE FUN FACTS

FACT: THE UNICORN IS THE NATIONAL ANIMAL OF SCOTLAND

IGNORE IF YOU'RE COLORING WITH MARKERS.

IF NOT, TAKE A BREAK WITH THESE FUN FACTS

FACT: HOT WATER AND COLD WATER SOUND DIFFERENT WHEN BEING POURED

IGNORE IF YOU'RE COLORING WITH MARKERS.

IF NOT, TAKE A BREAK WITH THESE FUN FACTS

FACT: A TICK BITE CAN MAKE YOU ALLERGIC TO RED MEAT

IGNORE IF YOU'RE COLORING WITH MARKERS.

IF NOT, TAKE A BREAK WITH THESE FUN FACTS

FACT: SWEAT DOESN'T ACTUALLY STINK

IGNORE IF YOU'RE COLORING WITH MARKERS.

IF NOT, TAKE A BREAK WITH THESE FUN FACTS

FACT: SHARKS CAN LIVE FOR FIVE CENTURIES

IGNORE IF YOU'RE COLORING WITH MARKERS.

IF NOT, TAKE A BREAK WITH THESE FUN FACTS

FACT: THE FIRE HYDRANT PATENT WAS LOST IN A FIRE

IGNORE IF YOU'RE COLORING WITH MARKERS.

IF NOT, TAKE A BREAK WITH THESE FUN FACTS

FACT:
ONE MAN ONCE SURVIVED TWO ATOMIC BOMBS

IGNORE IF YOU'RE COLORING WITH MARKERS.

IF NOT, TAKE A BREAK WITH THESE FUN FACTS

FACT: CHEETAHS CAN'T ROAR

IGNORE IF YOU'RE COLORING WITH MARKERS.

IF NOT, TAKE A BREAK WITH THESE FUN FACTS

FACT: MOST PEOPLE BREAK UP ON MONDAYS

IGNORE IF YOU'RE COLORING WITH MARKERS.

IF NOT, TAKE A BREAK WITH THESE FUN FACTS

FACT:
YOU CAN ALWAYS "SEE" YOUR NOSE

IGNORE IF YOU'RE COLORING WITH MARKERS.

IF NOT, TAKE A BREAK WITH THESE FUN FACTS

FACT: A BOLT OF LIGHTNING IS 5 TIMES HOTTER THAN THE SUN

IGNORE IF YOU'RE COLORING WITH MARKERS.

IF NOT, TAKE A BREAK WITH THESE FUN FACTS

FACT: 99.9% OF ALL SPECIES THAT HAVE EVER LIVED ON EARTH ARE EXTINCT

IGNORE IF YOU'RE COLORING WITH MARKERS.

IF NOT, TAKE A BREAK WITH THESE FUN FACTS

FACT: THERE IS AN IMMORTAL JELLYFISH

IGNORE IF YOU'RE COLORING WITH MARKERS.

IF NOT, TAKE A BREAK WITH THESE FUN FACTS

FACT: BABY BLUE WHALES GROW 200 POUNDS PER DAY FOR THE FIRST YEAR THEY ARE ALIVE

IGNORE IF YOU'RE COLORING WITH MARKERS.

IF NOT, TAKE A BREAK WITH THESE FUN FACTS

FACT: SOME CATS ARE ALLERGIC TO PEOPLE

IGNORE IF YOU'RE COLORING WITH MARKERS.

IF NOT, TAKE A BREAK WITH THESE FUN FACTS

FACT: APPLE PIE ISN'T AMERICAN

IGNORE IF YOU'RE COLORING WITH MARKERS.

IF NOT, TAKE A BREAK WITH THESE FUN FACTS

FACT: THE LYREBIRD CAN MIMIC ANY SOUNDS IT HEARS

IGNORE IF YOU'RE COLORING WITH MARKERS.

IF NOT, TAKE A BREAK WITH THESE FUN FACTS

FACT: YOU NEED AROUND 700 GRAPES TO MAKE A BOTTLE OF WINE

IGNORE IF YOU'RE COLORING WITH MARKERS.

IF NOT, TAKE A BREAK WITH THESE FUN FACTS

FACT: A $1 BILL COSTS $0.05 TO MAKE

IGNORE IF YOU'RE COLORING WITH MARKERS.

IF NOT, TAKE A BREAK WITH THESE FUN FACTS

FACT: DOGS NOSES ARE WET TO HELP ABSORB SCENT CHEMICALS

IGNORE IF YOU'RE COLORING WITH MARKERS.

IF NOT, TAKE A BREAK WITH THESE FUN FACTS

FACT: CATS CAN ROTATE THEIR EARS 180 DEGREES

IGNORE IF YOU'RE COLORING WITH MARKERS.

IF NOT, TAKE A BREAK WITH THESE FUN FACTS

FACT: YOU SHOULD THROW AWAY THE COTTON IN YOUR MEDS. COTTON CAN COLLECT MOISTURE AND CAN MAKE YOUR PILLS DETERIORIATE FASTER

IGNORE IF YOU'RE COLORING WITH MARKERS.

IF NOT, TAKE A BREAK WITH THESE FUN FACTS

FACT: YOU'RE TALLER WHEN YOU WAKE UP

IGNORE IF YOU'RE COLORING WITH MARKERS.

IF NOT, TAKE A BREAK WITH THESE FUN FACTS

FACT: YOU CAN'T BREATHE AND SWALLOW AT THE SAME TIME

IGNORE IF YOU'RE COLORING WITH MARKERS.

IF NOT, TAKE A BREAK WITH THESE FUN FACTS

FACT: IF YOU'RE CRAVING ICE, IT'S LIKELY YOU HAVE IRON DEFICIENCY

IGNORE IF YOU'RE COLORING WITH MARKERS.
IF NOT, TAKE A BREAK WITH THESE FUN FACTS

FACT: THE WIND IS SILENT UNTIL IT BLOWS AGAINST SOMETHING